Woodlands
IN CROSS STITCH

Angela Beazley

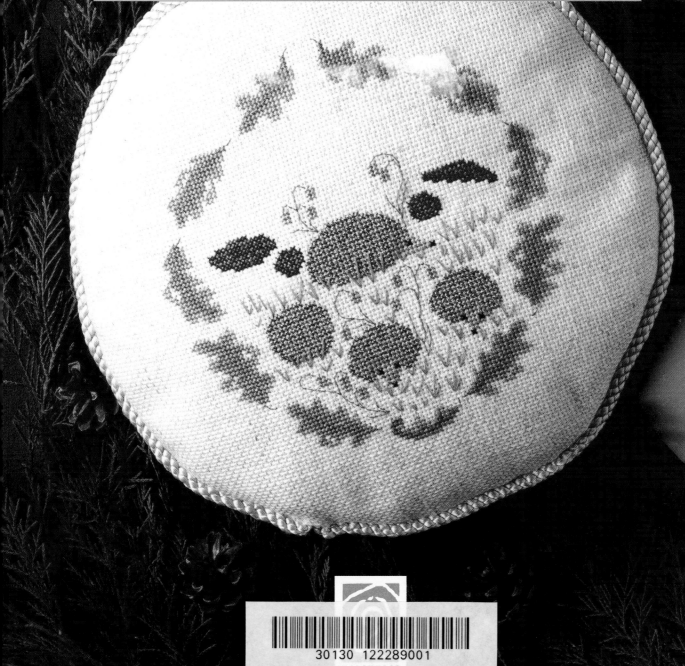

D0549620

30130 122289001

To Steph, Barry, Laurie and Tom,
with love and best wishes for the future.

THE CHARTS

Some of the designs in this book are very detailed and, due to inevitable space limitations, the charts may be shown on a comparatively small scale; in such cases, readers may find it helpful to have the particular chart with which they are currently working enlarged.

THREADS

The projects in this book were all stitched with DMC stranded cotton embroidery threads. The keys given with each chart also list thread combinations for those who wish to use Anchor or Madeira threads. It should be pointed out that the shades produced by different companies vary slightly, and it is not always possible to find identical colours in a different range.

Published in 1997 by Merehurst Limited
Ferry House, 51-57 Lacy Road, Putney, London SW15 1PR
Copyright © 1997 Merehurst Limited
ISBN 1 85391 526 2

All rights reserved. No part of this publication may be reproduced, stored in a retrieval system, or transmitted in any form or by any means, electronic, mechanical, photocopying, recording or otherwise, without the prior written permission of the copyright owner.

A catalogue record for this book is available from the British Library.

Edited by Heather Dewhurst
Designed by Maggie Aldred
Photography by Juliet Piddington
Illustrations by John Hutchinson and King & King (p14)
Typesetting by Dacorum Type & Print, Hemel Hempstead
Colour separation by Fotographics Limited, UK – Hong Kong
Printed in Hong Kong by Wing King Tong

Merehurst is the leading publisher of craft books and has an excellent range of titles to suit all levels. Please send to the address above for our free catalogue, stating the title of this book.

CONTENTS

INTRODUCTION

This little book is overflowing with the life and colour of the woodlands. The richness of trees in their summer foliage is complemented by the colour of the wild flowers which carpet the forest floor. The woodland birds and animals are brightly depicted in their natural habitat to bring the mystery of the quiet woods into your home.

The projects have been carefully designed to appeal to all ages, and all experience levels, many using beads and special sparkling threads to increase the dramatic element. Each project is beautifully illustrated with a full- colour picture, accompanied by clear charts and full details for completing each of the cross stitch items.

Cross stitch is extremely easy to do and, with help from the Basic Skills section of the book, even complete beginners will find many of the designs well within their scope.

For the dedicated cross stitcher, and the beginner alike, there is inspiration and variety for everyone. I hope that you enjoy selecting and stitching the items in this book as much as I enjoyed designing and making them.

Happy Stitching!

BASIC SKILLS

BEFORE YOU BEGIN

PREPARING THE FABRIC

Even with an average amount of handling, many evenweave fabrics tend to fray at the edges, so it is a good idea to overcast the raw edges, using ordinary sewing thread, before you begin.

FABRIC

Most of the projects in this book use 14-count Aida fabric, which has a surface of 14 clearly defined squares or 'blocks' of thread per 2.5cm (1in). Another fabric used is 27-count Linda; this fabric is evenweave, having the same number of warp and weft threads per 2.5cm (1in), and stitches are taken over two threads in each direction. Both of these fabrics are produced by Zweigart.

THE INSTRUCTIONS

Each project begins with a full list of the materials that you will require. The measurements given for the embroidery fabric include a minimum of 5cm (2in) all around to allow for stretching it in a frame and preparing the edges to prevent them from fraying.

Colour keys for stranded embroidery cottons – DMC, Anchor or Madeira – are given with each chart. It is assumed that you will need to buy one skein of each colour mentioned in a particular key, even though you may use less, but where two or more skeins are needed, this information is included in the main list of requirements.

Before you begin to embroider, always mark the centre of the design with two lines of basting stitches, one vertical and one horizontal, running from edge to edge of the fabric, as indicated by the arrows on the charts.

As you stitch, use the centre lines given on the chart and the basting threads on your fabric as reference points for counting the squares and threads to position your design accurately.

WORKING IN A HOOP

A hoop is the most popular frame for use with small areas of embroidery. It consists of two rings, one fitted inside the other; the outer ring usually has an adjustable screw attachment so that it can be tightened to hold the stretched fabric in place. Hoops are available in several sizes, ranging from 10cm (4in) in diameter to quilting hoops with a diameter of 38cm (15in). Hoops with table stands or floor stands attached are also available.

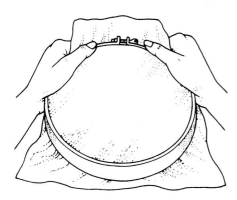

1 To stretch your fabric in a hoop, place the area to be embroidered over the inner ring and press the outer ring over it, with the tension screw released. Tissue paper can be placed between the outer ring and the embroidery, so that the hoop does not mark the fabric. Lay the tissue paper over the fabric when you set it in the hoop, then tear away the central embroidery area.

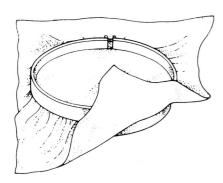

2 Smooth the fabric and, if necessary, straighten the grain before tightening the screw. The fabric should be evenly stretched.

WORKING IN A RECTANGULAR FRAME

Rectangular frames are more suitable for larger pieces of embroidery. They consist of two rollers, with tapes attached, and two flat side pieces, which slot into the rollers and are held in place by pegs or screw attachments. Available in different sizes, either alone or with adjustable table or floor stands, frames are measured by the length of the roller tape, and range in size from 30cm (12in) to 68cm (27in).

As alternatives to a slate frame, canvas stretchers and the backs of old picture frames can be used. Provided there is sufficient extra fabric around the finished size of the embroidery, the edges can be turned under and simply attached with drawing pins (thumb tacks) or staples.

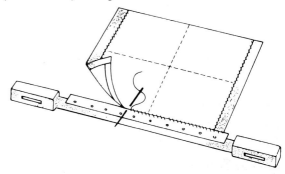

1 To stretch your fabric in a rectangular frame, cut out the fabric, allowing at least an extra 5cm (2in) all around the finished size of the embroidery. Baste a single 12mm (½in) turning on the top and bottom edges and oversew strong tape, 2.5cm (1in) wide, to the other two sides. Mark the centre line both ways with basting stitches. Working from the centre outwards and using strong thread, oversew the top and bottom edges to the roller tapes. Fit the side pieces into the slots, and roll any extra fabric on one roller until the fabric is taut.

2 Insert the pegs or adjust the screw attachments to secure the frame. Thread a large-eyed needle (chenille needle) with strong thread or fine string and lace both edges, securing the ends around the intersections of the frame. Lace the webbing at 2.5cm (1in) intervals, stretching the fabric evenly.

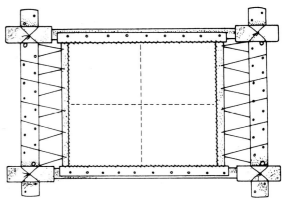

EXTENDING EMBROIDERY FABRIC

It is easy to extend a piece of embroidery fabric, such as a bookmark, to stretch it in a hoop.

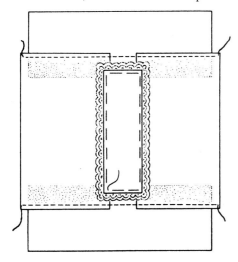

● Fabric oddments of a similar weight can be used. Simply cut four pieces to size (in other words, to the measurement that will fit both the embroidery fabric and your hoop) and baste them to each side of the embroidery fabric before stretching it in the hoop in the usual way.

THE STITCHES

CROSS STITCH

For all cross stitch embroidery, the following two methods of working are used. In each case, neat rows of vertical stitches are produced on the back of the fabric.

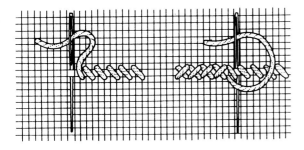

● When stitching large areas, work in horizontal rows. Working from right to left, complete the first row of evenly spaced diagonal stitches over the number of threads specified in the project instructions. Then, working from left to right, repeat the process. Continue in this way, making sure each stitch crosses in the same direction.

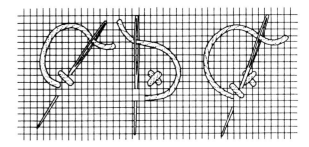

● When stitching diagonal lines, work downwards, completing each stitch before moving to the next. When starting a project always begin to embroider at the centre of the design and work outwards to ensure that the design will be placed centrally on the fabric.

BACKSTITCH

Backstitch is used in the projects to give emphasis to a particular foldline, an outline or a shadow. The stitches are worked over the same number of threads as the cross stitch, forming continuous straight or diagonal lines.

● Make the first stitch from left to right; pass the needle behind the fabric and bring it out one stitch length ahead to the left. Repeat and continue in this way along the line.

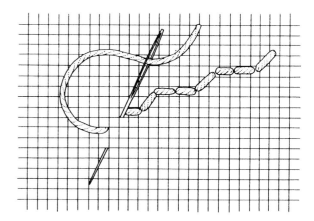

THREE-QUARTER CROSS STITCHES

Some fractional stitches are used on certain projects in this book; although they strike fear into the hearts of less experienced stitchers they are not difficult to master, and give a more natural line in certain instances. Should you find it difficult to pierce the centre of the Aida block, simply use a sharp needle to make a small hole in the centre first.

To work a three-quarter cross, bring the needle

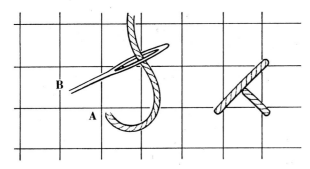

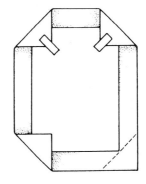

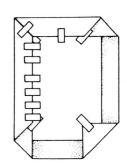

up at point A and down through the centre of the square at B. Later, the diagonal backstitch finishesthe stitch. A chart square with two different symbols separated by a diagonal line requires two 'three-quarter' stitches. Backstitch will later finish the square.

FRENCH KNOTS

This stitch is shown on some of the diagrams by a small circle. Where there are several french knots, the circles have been omitted to avoid confusion. Where this occurs you should refer to the instructions of the project and the colour photograph.

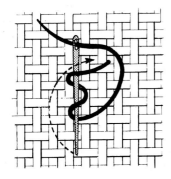

To work a french knot, bring your needle and cotton out slightly to the right of where you want your knot to be. Wind the thread once or twice around the needle, depending on how big you want your knot to be, and insert the needle to the left of the point where you brought it out.

Be careful not to pull too hard or the knot will disappear through the fabric. The instructions state the number of strands of cotton to be used for the french knots.

FINISHING

MOUNTING EMBROIDERY

The cardboard should be cut to the size of the finished embroidery, with an extra 6mm (¼in) added all round to allow for the recess in the frame.

1 Place embroidery face down, with the cardboard centred on top, and basting and pencil lines matching. Begin by folding over the fabric at each corner and securing it with masking tape.

2 Working first on one side and then the other, fold over the fabric on all sides and secure it firmly with pieces of masking tape, placed about 2.5cm (1in) apart. Also neaten the mitred corners with masking tape, pulling the fabric tightly to give a firm, smooth finish.

HEAVIER FABRICS

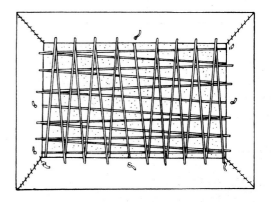

● Lay the embroidery face down, with the cardboard centred on top; fold over the edges of the fabric on opposite sides, making mitred folds at the corners, and lace across, using strong thread. Repeat on the other two sides. Finally, pull up the fabric firmly over the cardboard. Overstitch the mitred corners.

Bluebell Wood

In this delightful cross stitch picture we are led along a winding path into the heart of the bluebell wood. The rich purple carpet of flowers contrasts strongly with the green foliage of late spring beech trees.

BLUEBELL WOOD

YOU WILL NEED

For the Picture, with a design area measuring
15cm × 21.5cm (6in × 8¼in):

*33cm × 38cm (13¼in × 15¼in) of flecked blue/grey,
14-count Yorkshire Aida fabric
Stranded embroidery cotton in the colours given in
the panel
No24 or 26 tapestry needle
Strong thread, for lacing across the back
Cardboard, for mounting
Frame of your choice*

•

THE EMBROIDERY

Prepare the fabric, basting the horizontal and vertical centre lines, following the instructions given on page 4. Set the fabric in a hoop or frame, and begin stitching from the centre, following the chart. Ensure that the long axis of the fabric is running vertically.

Work the cross stitch using two strands of thread in the needle. Make sure that all the top stitches run in the same direction. Work the backstitch using one strand of thread.

FINISHING

Remove the embroidery from the frame. Gently hand wash the finished piece if necessary. Press on the reverse side with a warm steam iron. Stretch and mount the embroidery as explained on page 7. Insert the mounted picture into the frame, and assemble the frame according to the manufacturer's instructions.

BLUEBELL WOOD ▶	DMC	ANCHOR	MADEIRA
A Pale purple	340	118	0803
B Mid purple	3746	1030	0804
C Dark purple	333	119	0713
K Dark stone	3032	392	2002
D Light dull brown	640	393	1905
L Dull brown	611	889	2107
E Dark dull brown	610	905	2106
2 Light yellow-green	471	265	1501
1 Medium stone	612	898	2108
S Dark green	3345	268	1406
T Medium green	3346	267	1407
V Light green	3347	266	1408
H Light stone	613	853	2109

Note: bks bluebell stems in dark green.

TOP

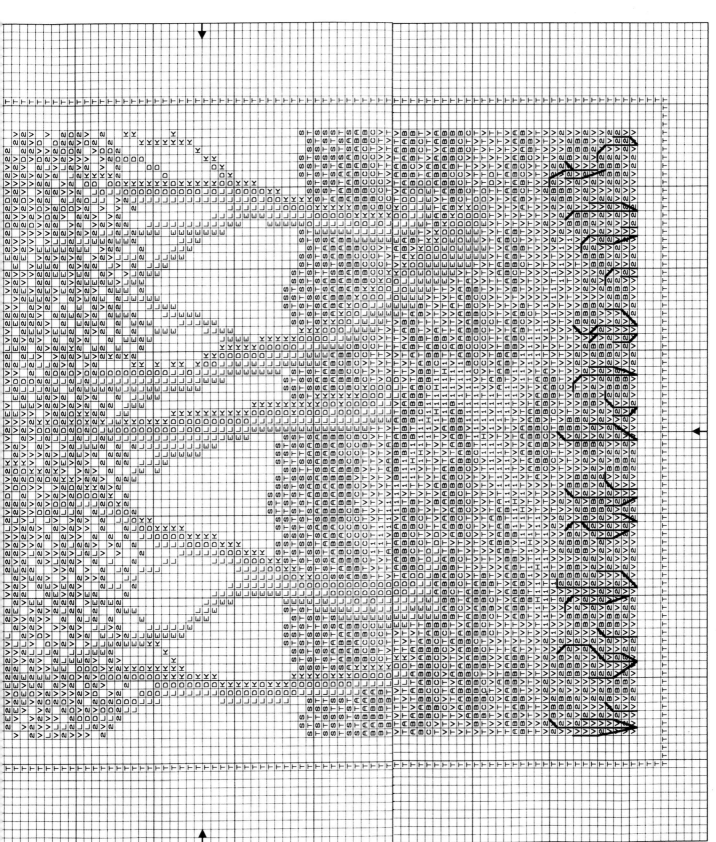

Forest at Night

The mystery of the forest at night
with all its dark enchantment
is recreated in this cross
stitch picture. Under a sparkling
full moon badgers feed quietly,
while the owl hunts among
the treetops.

FOREST AT NIGHT

YOU WILL NEED

For the Picture, with a design area of
15.5cm × 20cm (6¼in × 8in):

*30cm × 35cm (12in × 14in) of teal green,
14-count Aida fabric
Stranded embroidery cotton in the colours given in
the panel
No24 or 26 tapestry needle
Anchor Marlitt rayon threads in the colours given in
the panel
Anchor Ophir gold thread
Bead Design seed beads in the colours given in
the panel
Astrella gold thread
Beading needle
Strong thread, for lacing across the back
Cardboard, for mounting
Frame of your choice*

•

THE EMBROIDERY

Prepare the fabric, basting the horizontal and
vertical centre lines, following the instructions
given on page 4. Set the fabric in a hoop or frame,
and begin stitching from the centre, following
the chart. Ensure that the long axis of the fabric is
running vertically.

Work the cross stitch using two strands of
thread in the needle. Then work the backstitch and
long straight stitches with two strands of thread in
the needle. Next, work the french knots with two
strands of thread in the needle. Refer to the colour
photograph for the position of the french knots.
For the gold cross stitch moon use the Ophir
bright gold thread with one strand in the needle,
and the Astrella light gold with two strands in the
needle. Work the clouds with one strand of cotton,
and stitching only the second half of the cross stitch
(a diagonal stitch).

Stitch the beads on with the beading needle,
using green thread as follows. Stitch the beads on
to the embroidery after you have finished all the
cross stitch and backstitch, to prevent the beads
breaking in the embroidery hoop. Using a beading
needle, stitch beads on with a diagonal stitch, using
the direction of the second half of a cross stitch (see
the diagram).

BEADING

FINISHING

Remove the embroidery from the frame. Gently hand
wash the finished piece if necessary. Press on the
reverse side with a warm steam iron. Stretch and
mount the embroidery as explained on page 7. Insert
the mounted picture into the frame, and assemble the
frame according to the manufacturer's instructions.

FOREST AT NIGHT ▶	DMC	ANCHOR	MADEIRA
A Dark avocado	3012	854	1606
3 Dark sand	420	375	2104
4 Rusty brown	434	310	2009
8 Light avocado	371	945	1605
9 Apple green	3347	266	1408
D Golden brown	435	365	2010
⊠ Light stone	738	361	2013
H Dark rich brown	801	359	2007
L Very dark grey	3799	236	1809
P Dark green	3346	267	1407
N Dark grey	413	400	1713
E Pale grey	415	398	1803
Very dark brown*	3031	360	2003
Light green*	470	261	1502
○ Bright pink+	3687	68	0506
○ Bright yellow+		Marlitt 867	Decora yellow
B Rust		1040	chocolate
2 Dark green		1032	hunter green
5 Bright green		1030	dark avocado
C Dark grey		870	dark grey
◇ Black		801	black
▱ White		800	white
W Light gold	Argent	Effektgarn	No15 shade 22
6 Bright gold		Ophir	No15 Shade 27
☒ Pale green seed bead			Bead Design Shade 36

Note: bks the tree stems with very dark brown, and the flower stems
with light green* (*used for backstitch only). Work the pink flowers
with french knots in bright pink+, and the yellow flowers in bright
yellow+.*

Wild Flowers and Butterflies

In this design, bright butterflies are
busy gathering nectar among the
woodland flowers. The subtle colours
of honeysuckle are intertwined with
dark beaded blackberries.

WILD FLOWERS
AND BUTTERFLIES

YOU WILL NEED

For the Table Runner, with a design area of
16.5cm × 24cm (6½in × 9½in), and a finished size of
25.5cm × 35.5cm (10¼in × 14¼in)
excluding fringe:

*50cm × 45cm (20in × 18in) of white,
27-count evenweave fabric
Stranded embroidery cotton in the colours given in
the panel
No24 or 26 tapestry needle
Bead Design beads, in the colours given in the panel
Beading needle
White stranded cotton for hemstitching the edges*

●

THE EMBROIDERY

Prepare the fabric, basting the horizontal and vertical centre lines, following the instructions given on page 4. Set the fabric in a hoop or frame, and begin stitching from the centre, following the chart. Ensure that the long axis of the fabric is running horizontally.

Work the cross stitch using two strands of thread in the needle. Work the backstitch with one strand of stranded cotton, following the chart key. Work the last stitch four times in each case. Work the beads with one strand of thread in the beading needle, using the nearest colour thread to the bead in each case. Attach the beads with a diagonal stitch, making sure all the beads lie in the same direction as the second half of the cross stitches (see page 14).

FINISHING

Remove the embroidery from the frame. Work the hem in the following way. Keeping the embroidery centred, measure to the hem edge (25.5cm × 35.5cm/10¼in × 14¼in) and withdraw a thread on all sides. Using two strands of white stranded cotton in the tapestry needle, and taking each stitch around four threads of the fabric, hemstitch around the table runner, along the hemline. Bring the needle out on the right side of the work, two threads below the drawn-thread line. Working from left to right, pick up threads. Bring the needle out again and insert it behind the fabric to emerge two threads down, ready to make the next stitch. Before inserting the needle pull the thread tight, so that the bound threads form a neat group.

When you have finished, carefully trim away the excess fabric, leaving a fringe of 2cm (¾in) all the way around. Remove the excess threads of the fabric below the hemstitching.

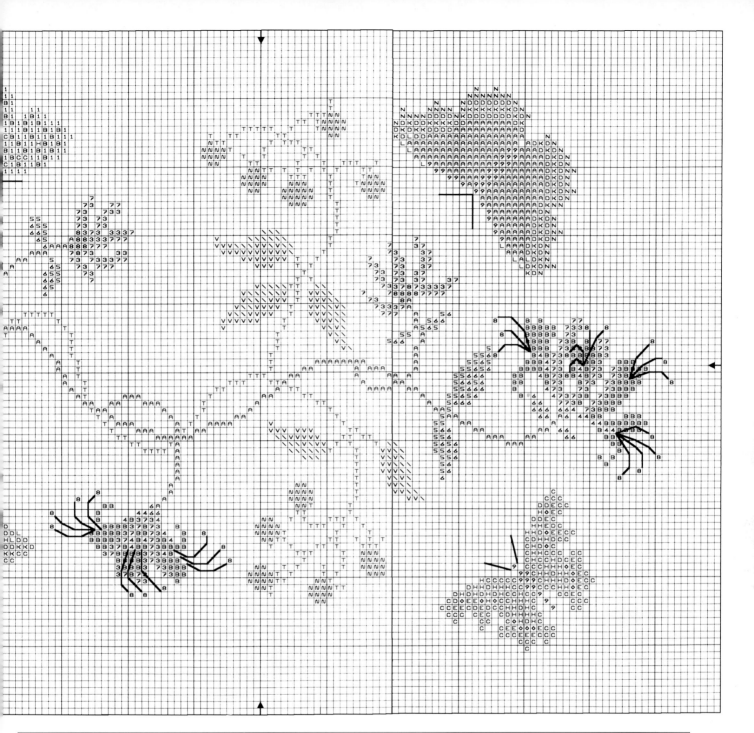

WILD FLOWERS AND BUTTERFLIES

		DMC	ANCHOR	MADEIRA			DMC	ANCHOR	MADEIRA
A	Maroon	3802	1019	0810	H	Golden brown	3826	1049	2306
B	Yellow	727	293	0110	◇	Reddish-brown	975	310	2303
1	Dark yellow	726	295	0100	K	Purple	3746	1030	0803
3	Medium pink	316	969	0809	N	Light yellow	745	300	0111
4	Light pink	3727	1016	0808	L	Ecru	Ecru	Ecru	Ecru
5	Dark green	3346	267	1407	＼	Brownish-green	830	906	2114
6	Light green	3347	266	1408	∧	Dark grey	3787	904	1809
7	Light red	3726	1018	0812	T	Dark greyish-green	936	846	1507
9	Dark brown	3781	1050	0813	V	Yellowish-green	732	281	1612
C	Light brown	640	393	1905	8	Pink seed bead		Bead Design Shade 232	
D	Black	310	403	Black	N	Blackberry seed bead		Bead Design Shade 64	
E	Orange	976	0309	2302					

Note: bks the diagonal butterfly antennae with dark brown, and the honeysuckle stamens with light green.

Hedgehog Cushion

A mother hedgehog and her babies are feeding under the shade of brightly coloured mushrooms on this decorative little stitched cushion. The garland of tumbling autumn oak leaves frames the charming scene.

HEDGEHOG CUSHION

For the Cushion, with a design area of
18cm (7$\frac{1}{4}$in) in diameter, and a finished size of
28cm (11$\frac{1}{4}$in):

*38cm (15$\frac{1}{4}$in) square of gold-flecked oatmeal,
14-count Aida fiddler cloth
Stranded embroidery cotton in the colours given in
the panel
No24 or 26 tapestry needle
Anchor Marlitt rayon embroidery threads in the
colours given in the panel
Pair of compasses and pencil
Matching fabric for back of cushion
Matching sewing thread
28cm (11$\frac{1}{4}$in) circular cushion pad
Piping cord*

•

THE EMBROIDERY

Prepare the fabric, basting the horizontal and
vertical centre lines, following the instructions
given on page 4. Set the fabric in a hoop or frame,
and begin stitching from the centre of the design,
following the chart opposite.

Work the cross stitch using two strands of thread
in the needle. Make sure the top stitches all run in
the same direction. Work the backstitch as follows.
Work the bluebell stems and the leaf stems with one
strand of cotton, and work the grasses with two
strands of cotton (refer to the chart key for specific
instructions).

FINISHING

Remove the embroidery from the frame. Gently hand
wash if necessary. Press on the reverse side with a
warm steam iron. Carefully centring the embroidery,
mark a circle on the reverse of the fabric with a
sharp, hard pencil, outlining the cushion size
(28cm/11$\frac{1}{4}$in circle). Use a pair of compasses to
draw the line.

Place the cushion front and back together, with
right sides facing, and machine stitch around the
edge, along the pencil line. Leave a 20cm (8in)
opening at the bottom of the design. Snip away the
excess fabric, leaving a seam allowance of 2cm

(¾in). Neaten the edges with an overlocker, or
machine zigzag stitch. Turn the cushion cover right
side out, and insert the cushion pad. Slipstitch the
opening to reduce it to 2cm (¾in). Slipstitch piping
cord around the seam, tucking the ends into the
small opening, before slipstitching this closed.

HEDGEHOG ▶ CUSHION	DMC	ANCHOR	MADEIRA
C Light golden brown	436	363	2011
B Dark golden brown	434	310	2009
A Medium golden brown	435	365	2010
2 Dark red	817	47	0211
3 Red	350	011	0213
4 White	White	White	White
5 Cream	3770	1009	0306
6 Black	310	403	Black
9 Purple	340	118	0803
7 Golden brown		Marlitt 1039	Decora 869
with dark grey	413	400	1713
8 Light golden brown	436	363	2011
with medium grey	414	399	1801
Green*	469	267	1503
Light green*	3347	266	1408

Note: bks the bluebell stems with green, the grasses with light green*,
(*used for backstitch only), and the leaf stems with dark golden brown.*

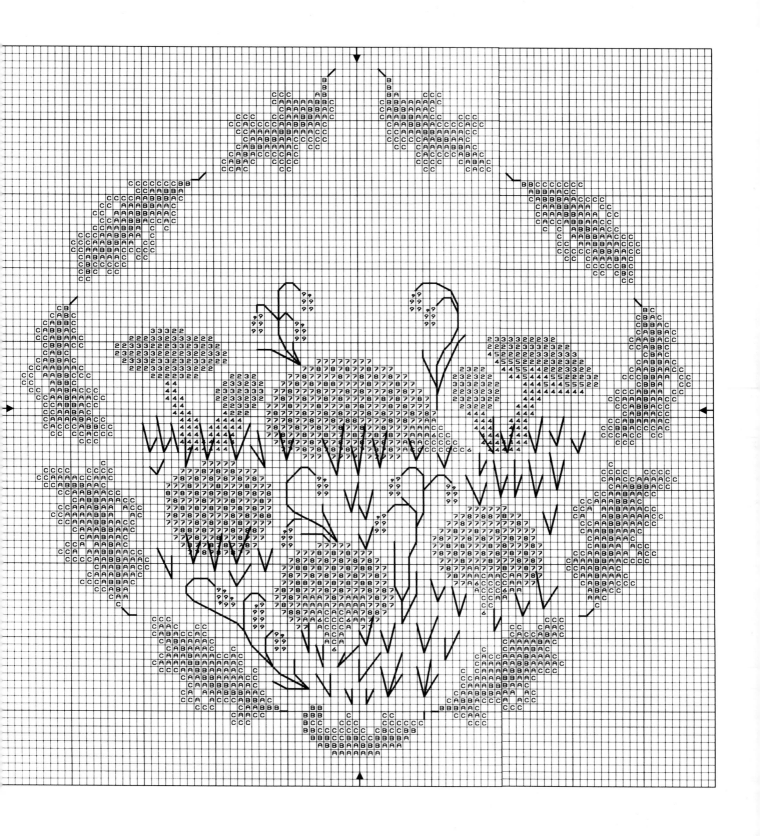

Woodland Sampler

This traditional sampler, with its floral border of primroses and bluebells, depicts life in the woodlands. From birds to butterflies, wild flowers to wild animals, all the woodland favourites are here in one design.

WOODLAND SAMPLER

For the Sampler, with a design area of
20cm × 24cm (8in × 9½in):

*35cm × 38cm (14in × 15¼in) of dark ecru,
14-count Aida fabric
Stranded embroidery cotton in the colours given in
the panel
No24 or 26 tapestry needle
Bead Design seed beads in the colours given in
the panel
Beading needle
Strong thread, for lacing across the back
Cardboard for mounting
Frame of your choice*

●

THE EMBROIDERY

Prepare the fabric, basting the horizontal and
vertical centre lines, following the instructions
given on page 4. Set the fabric in a hoop or frame,
and begin stitching from the centre, following
the chart. Ensure that the long axis of the fabric is
running vertically.

Work the cross stitch using two strands of thread
in the needle. Make sure all the top stitches run in
the same direction. Stitch the beads with a diagonal
stitch, using the direction of the second half of a
cross stitch. Use the beading needle, and match the
colour of thread as closely as possible (see page 14).

Work the backstitch with one or two strands of
thread, referring to the chart key.

FINISHING

Remove the embroidery from the frame. Gently hand
wash the finished piece if necessary. Press on the
reverse side with a warm steam iron. Stretch and
mount the embroidery as explained on page 7.

Insert the mounted picture into the frame, and
assemble according to the manufacturer's instructions.

WOODLAND ▶ SAMPLER		DMC	ANCHOR	MADEIRA
⌐	Reddish-brown	400	351	2305
C	Brown	433	358	2008
V	Dark reddish-brown	301	349	2306
T	Light tan	3826	1049	2302
A	Golden brown	435	365	2010
•	White	White	White	White
■	Black	310	0403	Black
▲	Very dark brown	3031	360	2003
B	Ecru	Ecru	Ecru	Ecru
P	Flesh pink	3779	868	0304
S	Light yellow	727	293	0110
K	Bright yellow	726	295	0100
I	Apple green	988	257	1402
2	Dark apple green	987	258	1403
∧	Purple	340	118	0803
◇	Light green	3347	266	1408
3	Medium green	3346	267	1407
N	Stone	612	898	2108
Z	Light stone	3032	392	2002
H	Avocado	3012	854	1606
4	Dull brown	420	375	2104
6	Light grey	647	1040	1813
7	Golden sand	436	363	2011
8	Light yellowish-green	471	265	1501
9	Dark green	3345	268	1406
O	Dark blue	791	127	0904
X	Blue	792	941	905
+	Grey	646	8581	1812
=	Dark yellow	725	297	0108
I	Pale yellow seed bead		Bead Design Shade 80	
⊥	Orange seed bead		Bead Design Shade 51	
	Pine green*	501	878	1704

Note: bks violet stems with two strands of medium green; outline deer, fox, red squirrel, owl and log with one strand of very dark brown; mushroom stems with two strands of stone; grass under mushrooms with two strands of light green; grass under fox with two strands of apple green; honeysuckle flowers and oak leaves with one strand of light green; pine needles with one strand of pine green* (*used for backstitch only); and butterfly with one strand of grey.

Woodland Bird Bell Pull

The colourful plumage of the green woodpecker, the nuthatch and the tree creeper combines with the twinning ivy on this tree to create a pretty bell pull.

WOODLAND
BIRD BELL PULL

YOU WILL NEED

For the Bell Pull, with a design area of
10cm × 39cm (4in × 15¹/₂in), and a finished size of
10cm × 41.5cm (4in × 16³/₈in):

*23cm × 50cm (9¹/₄in × 20in) of dark ecru,
14-count Aida fabric
Stranded embroidery cotton in the colours given in
the panel
No24 or 26 tapestry needle
Two 10cm (4in) bell pull ends
Matching backing fabric
Matching sewing thread and needle*

•

THE EMBROIDERY

Prepare the fabric, basting the horizontal and
vertical centre lines, following the instructions
given on page 4. Set the fabric in a hoop or frame,
and begin stitching the design from the centre,
following the chart below. Ensure that the long axis
of the fabric runs vertically.

Work the cross stitch using two strands of thread
in the needle. Make sure that all the top stitches run
in the same direction. Work the backstitch with one
strand of thread in the needle for the bird outlines,
and two strands for the birds' feet.

FINISHING

Remove the embroidery from the frame. Gently hand
wash the finished piece if necessary. Press on the
reverse side with a warm steam iron.

Centring the embroidery carefully, measure 10cm
(4in) across the bell pull and turn the long edges
under and press. Leave an allowance of 2.5cm (1in)
at the top and bottom and press. Leaving a seam
allowance of 2cm (³/₄in), trim away excess fabric on
all four sides.

Mitre the corners as follows. Press a single hem
to the wrong side, the same as the measurement
given in the instructions. Open the hem out again
and fold the corner of the fabric inwards, as shown
on the diagram. Refold the hem to the wrong
side along the pressed line, and slipstitch in place.
Press to neaten.

Place the bell pull ends onto the embroidery and
baste the top and bottom edges in place. Prepare the
backing fabric in the same way and slipstitch into
place using matching sewing thread. Remove the
basting thread and press lightly on the reverse side.

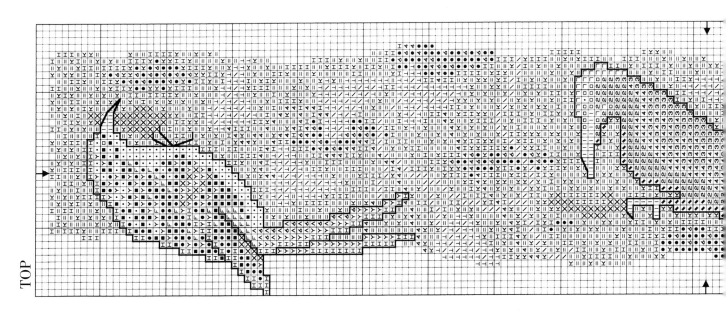

TOP

MITRING A CORNER

WOODLAND BIRD ▼ BELL PULL		DMC	ANCHOR	MADEIRA
⊓	Red	349	13	212
I	Dark greyish-brown	3787	904	1809
2	Greenish-yellow	734	279	1610
⧅	Dark greenish-yellow	733	280	1611
3	Apple green	470	264	1502
4	Dark apple green	471	265	1501
Y	Medium brown	840	379	1912
X	Very dark brown	3021	905	1904
P	Yellow	726	295	0100
H	Brown	839	380	1913
∧	Light rust	436	1363	2011
⧄	Light green	3347	266	1408
⊥	Medium green	3346	267	1407
=	Stone	612	898	2108
K	Dark stone	611	889	2107
6	Dark rust	435	365	2010
F	Golden sand	437	362	2012
•	Ecru	Ecru	Ecru	Ecru
A	Blue	931	921	1711
B	Light blue	932	920	1710
T	Dark blue	3750	1036	1005
C	Orange	922	337	0310
E	Light orange	402	347	2307
S	Pale grey	415	398	1803
V	Flesh	3774	778	0305
☐	Black	310	0403	Black
■	Dull brown	3790	393	1905
●	Tan	420	375	2104
	Very dark grey*	3799	236	1713

Note: bks bird outlines and birds' feet with very dark grey* (*used for backstitch only).

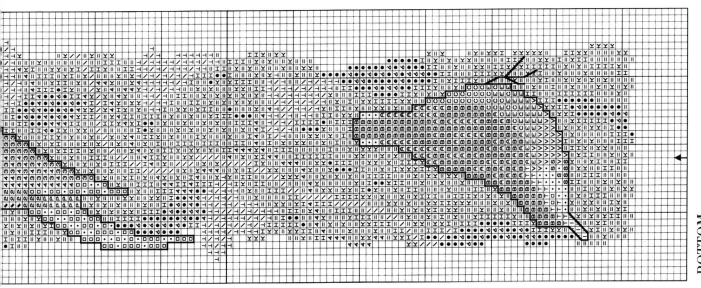

BOTTOM

Sleeping Wood Nymph

This little nymph is curled up fast
asleep in a crab apple tree.
The magical qualities of her wings
are created by blending gold and
silver threads with beads.

SLEEPING WOOD NYMPH

YOU WILL NEED

For the Nightdress Case with a design area of 21cm × 15cm (8³/₈in × 6in), and a finished size of 27cm × 24cm (10³/₄in × 9¹/₂in) excluding frill:

45cm (18in) square of flecked blue/grey, 14-count Yorkshire Aida fabric
Stranded embroidery cotton in the colours given in the panel
No24 or 26 tapestry needle
Stranded gold and silver thread
Bead Design beads in the colours given in the panel
Beading needle
Lace frill for trimming
Backing fabric
Matching sewing thread
Two 50cm (20in) lengths of white satin ribbon, 12mm (¹/₂in) wide

•

THE EMBROIDERY

Prepare the fabric, basting the horizontal and vertical centre lines, following the instructions given on page 4. Set the fabric in a frame or hoop, and begin stitching from the centre, following the chart.

Work the cross stitch using two strands of thread in the needle. Work the nymph's wings as follows. Work the first half of the cross stitch with one strand of gold thread, and complete the stitch with one strand of silver thread. Make sure that all the top stitches run in the same direction.

Work the backstitch with one strand of stranded cotton. Attach the beads with the beading needle, using the closest match of stranded cotton (see page 14).

FINISHING

Remove the embroidery from the frame. Gently hand wash the finished piece if necessary. Press on the reverse side with a warm steam iron.

Make up the nightdress case as follows. Centre the design carefully and pin out a rectangle measuring 27cm × 24cm (10³/₄in × 9¹/₂in). Allowing a further 2cm (³/₄in) seam allowance beyond this, trim away the excess fabric. Pin and baste a lace frill onto the front panel, making three small pleats in the corners. Press the frill towards the centre of the design.

Cut the backing piece in two and hem along one of the long sides on each piece. Place these on a table with right sides facing and hemmed edges together. Slide the left-hand piece over the right-hand piece so that they overlap by 7cm (2³/₄in). Pin in place to make a rectangle 27cm × 24cm (10³/₄in × 9¹/₂in). Trim away the excess fabric to match the front piece. Baste along the overlap at top and bottom. With right sides together, place the backing pieces and the front piece together and carefully stitch a seam around the edges, making sure that the lace frill is trapped in the seam. Neaten the edges. Slipstitch a white ribbon onto each side of the back of the completed nightdress case, on either side of the opening, to form a tie.

WOOD NYMPH ▲	DMC	ANCHOR	MADEIRA
⬛O Brown	610	905	2106
⬛N Dark avocado green	3011	856	1607
· White	White	White	White
⬛P Pale pink	3713	1020	0503
⬛C Yellow	3822	295	0109
⬛1 Light green	471	265	1501
⬛2 Dark green	3347	266	1408
⬛3 Flesh	951	880	2308
⬛5 Dark reddish-brown	433	358	2008
⬛6 Light reddish-brown	434	310	2009
⬛∧ Dark pink	224	894	0813
⬛∟ Medium pink	223	895	0812
⬛✓ Gold	Argent Cristallina 300 No15, shade 22		
⬛✓ Silver	Or Cristallina 301 No15, silver		
⬛◇ Pale pink seed bead	Bead Design Shade 54		
Donkey brown*	840	379	1912

Note: bks flower stems with dark green, the wood nymph's mouth with medium pink, and the outline of the face with donkey brown* (*used for backstitch only).

Woodland Deer Cushion

At the edge of the woodland stand two watchful deer. Framed by the trees of the forest, they are depicted beside the soft pinks of wild flowers.

WOODLAND DEER CUSHION

YOU WILL NEED

For the Cushion, with a design area of 32cm (12³/₄in) square, and a finished size of 38cm (15³/₄in) square:

50cm (20in) square of white, 27-count evenweave fabric
Stranded embroidery cotton in the colours given in the panel
No24 or 26 tapestry needle
Matching backing fabric
Sewing thread
38cm (15¹/₄in) square cushion pad

•

THE EMBROIDERY

Prepare the fabric, basting the horizontal and vertical lines, following the instructions given on page 4. Set the fabric in a hoop or frame, and begin stitching from the centre, following the chart.

Work the cross stitch with two strands of stranded cotton. Make sure that all the top stitches run in the same direction. Work the backstitch with one strand of cotton.

FINISHING

Remove the embroidery from the frame. Gently hand wash the finished piece if necessary. Press on the reverse side with a warm steam iron.

Centre the design carefully. Measure the 38cm (15¹/₄in) square and pin the seam line on the front of the fabric. Allow a 2cm (³/₄in) seam allowance and trim away excess fabric carefully. With right sides together, pin and baste the seam line for the cushion back and front. Machine stitch around the seam line, leaving an opening of 23cm (9¹/₄in) in the centre of the lower edge. Neaten the raw edges. Turn the cover the right side out and place the cushion pad inside. Slipstich the opening closed.

DEER CUSHION ▶	DMC	ANCHOR	MADEIRA
2 Medium greyish-brown	3790	904	2107
A Light golden sand	435	365	2010
L Dark reddish-brown	400	351	2305
V Reddish-brown	301	349	2306
T Light reddish-brown	3826	1049	2302
▲ Dark brown	3031	360	2003
B Cream	3033	830	2001
6 Light pine green	3363	860	1402
7 Dark pine green	3362	861	1312
8 Light bright green	3347	266	1408
9 Dark bright green	3346	267	1407
1 Dark golden sand	420	375	2104
= Very pale pink	963	048	0608
Λ Pale pink	3326	026	0504
⋈ Medium greyish-green	368	0214	1310
◇ Pale greyish-green	320	0215	1311
И Bright pink	3806	062	0505
▽ Dark bright pink	3805	063	0506
╱ Light greyish-brown	640	393	1905

Note: bks the flower stems with light pine green, and around the deer with dark brown.

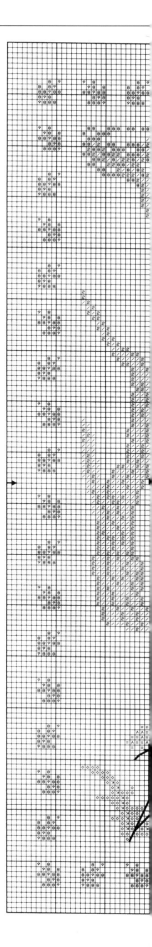

ACKNOWLEDGEMENTS

Many thanks to DMC for supplying the threads and Zweigart fabrics used throughout this book.

Thanks also the Coats Paton Crafts, for the Marlitt, Ophir and Astrella threads; Sew It All, for the Fiddler Cloth; Reflexions and Cross Purposes for the bell pull ends; Bead Design for the seed beads used in many of the projects; and Peter Hodson Frames for the Woodland Sampler frame.

SUPPLIERS

Sew It All
Garden Cottage
Oving
Buckinghamshire
Telephone: 01296 641524

Bead Design
35 March Road
Wimblington
March
Cambridgeshire
PE15 0RW
Telephone: 01354 740341

Reflexions and Cross Purposes
The Stables
Black Bull Yard
Welton
Lincolnshire
LN2 3HZ
Telephone: 01673 862717

Peter Hodson Frames
4 Butler Place
Cleethorpes
South Humberside
DN35 7SG
Telephone: 01472 355074

Addresses for Framecraft stockists worldwide
Framecraft Miniatures Limited
372/376 Summer Lane
Hockley
Birmingham B19 3QA
England
Telephone: 0121 359 4442

Ireland Needlecraft Pty Ltd
2-4 Keppel Drive
Hallam, Victoria 3803
Australia

Danish Art Needlework
PO Box 442, Lethbridge
Alberta T1J 3Z1
Canada

Sanyei Imports
PO Box 5, Hashima Shi
Gifu 501-62
Japan

The Embroidery Shop
286 Queen Street
Masterton
New Zealand

Anne Brinkley Designs Inc.
246 Walnut Street
Newton
Mass. 02160
USA

S A Threads and Cottons Ltd
43 Somerset Road
Cape Town
South Africa

For information on your nearest stockist of embroidery cotton, contact the following:

DMC
(also distributors of Zweigart fabrics)
UK
DMC Creative World Limited
62 Pullman Road, Wigston
Leicester LE8 2DY
Telephone: 01162 2811040

USA
The DMC Corporation
Port Kearney Bld.
10 South Kearney
NJ 07032-0650
Telephone: 201 589 0606

AUSTRALIA
DMC Needlecraft Pty
PO Box 317
Earlswood 2206
NSW 2204
Telephone: 02599 3088

COATS AND ANCHOR
UK
Coats Paton Crafts
McMullen Road
Darlington
Co. Durham DL1 1YQ
Telephone: 01325 381010

USA
Coats & Clark
PO Box 27067
Dept CO1
Greenville SC 29616
Telephone: 803 234 0103

AUSTRALIA
Coats Patons Crafts
Thistle Street
Launceston
Tasmania 7250
Telephone: 00344 4222

MADEIRA
UK
Madeira Threads (UK) Limited
Thirsk Industrial Park
York Road, Thirsk
N. Yorkshire YO7 3BX
Telephone: 01845 524880

USA
Madeira Marketing Limited
600 East 9th Street
Michigan City
IN 46360
Telephone: 219 873 1000

AUSTRALIA
Penguin Threads Pty Limited
25-27 Izett Street
Prahran
Victoria 3181
Telephone: 03529 4400